GOD,
I WON'T LET GO
UNTIL YOU
HEAL ME!

FAITH TO MOVE MOUNTAINS
OF SICKNESS AND DISEASE

Elaine B. Posey

WESTBOW
PRESS®
A DIVISION OF THOMAS NELSON
& ZONDERVAN

WestBow Press books may be ordered through booksellers or by contacting:

WestBow Press
A Division of Thomas Nelson & Zondervan
1663 Liberty Drive
Bloomington, IN 47403
www.westbowpress.com
844-714-3454

Scripture quotations are taken from the Holy Bible, King James Version.

ISBN: 979-8-3850-0290-0 (sc)
ISBN: 979-8-3850-0291-7 (e)

Library of Congress Control Number: 2023913034

Print information available on the last page.

WestBow Press rev. date: 08/22/2023

To my loving husband, Dr. James A. Posey III

He is truly a man of God who humbly wears a coat of many colors, a brilliant yet compassionate physician with a pastor's heart. He is the love of my life!

Thank you for supporting and believing in me.

All my love,

Elaine

Contents

Preface

"Mr. X or Miss Y, the test results indicate ..."

"Mr. T or Mrs. Z, your scan shows ..."

"The x-rays confirm ..."

"Ms. W, we need to run further tests ..."

It's that moment—the moment when you hear the official diagnosis for the first time. The knowledge is a relief to some because at least now they know what they're dealing with— they have a name for it. Knowing the name is important because now your enemy has been identified.

The Word tells us that there is no name higher than the name of our Lord. Bless that powerful name of Jesus Christ!

> Wherefore God also hath highly exalted him, and given him a name which is above every name: That at the name of Jesus every knee should bow, of things in heaven, and things in earth, and things under the earth. (Philippians 2:9–10)

The pronouncement of a diagnosis often causes one to be shocked, overwhelmed, fearful, or in a state of denial. I experienced all those emotions concerning my health and the health of some of my family members and close friends.

I was born with severe asthma. As an infant, I often was hospitalized because just about everything triggered an allergic reaction. The disease threatened my life several times with severe attacks, from birth to age two years. But God! In 2014, I was diagnosed with Parkinson's disease, a chronic degenerative neurologic disease with no known cure. In 2019, a routine eye exam discovered that I had developed holes in both retinas. I was legally blind. My only option was to undergo surgery as soon as possible or slowly go completely blind, with no chance of recovering my sight once it was lost.

Today, I'm healed, and I walk in divine health. But it has and still requires constant prayer and verbal profession of my faith. God blessed me with the faith to believe him for supernatural childbirths in 1993 and 1997 (no epidurals or general anesthesia)! I thank God for the gift of faith.

I wrote this book to share this priceless gift with you. God has called me to preach good tidings to the meek. He has sent me to bind up the broken-hearted, to proclaim liberty to the captives and the opening of the prison to them who are bound (Isaiah 61:1). Will you be made whole? Healing is available to all, and it manifests according to your faith!

CHAPTER 1

Faith Is Essential!

> But without faith it is impossible to please him:
> for he that cometh to God must believe that he is,
> and that he is a rewarder of them that diligently
> seek him. (Hebrews 11:6)

First things first: have you come to God? Have you fully surrendered and given your life to our Lord Jesus Christ? Jesus died on the cross to reconcile us back to the Father by taking our punishment for sin. Salvation is free and available to everyone, but even salvation requires a measure of faith to believe, accept, and begin to walk in it. If you do not know the Lord, I invite you to pray now and accept him into your heart.

Prayer for Salvation

> Heavenly Father, I come to you in the name of
> Jesus. Your Word says, "Whosoever shall call
> on the name of the Lord shall be saved" (Acts

2:21). I am calling on you. I pray and ask Jesus
to come into my heart and be Lord over my life,
according to Romans 10:9–10.

Faith Is Essential

Faith is the essential ingredient to receiving your healing and
maintaining divine health. Faith is the supernatural force
that powers the kingdom of God. By faith, the worlds were
framed, and without it, it is impossible to please God. Mark
11:22 admonishes us to have faith in God. Our faith fuels
the glory of God and releases miracles, signs, wonders, and
healings!

> And whatsoever ye shall ask in my name, that
> will I do, that the Father may be glorified in the
> Son. If ye shall ask any thing in my name, I will
> do it. (John 14:13–14)

It all begins with faith. Before any miracle is received or any
prayer is prayed, you must have faith in God.

> Now Faith is the substance of things hoped for,
> the evidence of things not seen. (Hebrews 11:1)

> In the beginning was the Word, and the Word
> was with God, and the Word was God. The same
> was in the beginning with God. All things were
> made by him; and without him was not anything
> made that was made. In him was life; and the
> life was the light of men. (John 1:1–4,)

God created man in his image (Genesis 1:27). We are fearfully, wonderfully, and intricately made (Psalm 139:14). God values and is aware of our bodies to the extent of numbering the hairs in our heads (Matthew 10:30)! God is meticulous and precise. His words are full of life. Proverbs 4:22 says, "For they are life unto those that find them, and health to all their flesh." Romans 10:17 tells us that "Faith comes by hearing, and hearing the Word of God." "Jesus said unto him, If thou canst believe, all things are possible to him that believeth" (Mark 9:23). When we ask in faith, God is faithful to reward us with the answers to our prayers. He commands us to "only believe" (Mark 5:36).

> Therefore; I say unto you, What things soever ye desire, when ye pray, believe that ye receive them, and ye shall have them. (Mark 11:24)

Since faith is essential, we must know what it is, how it works, and how to get it. The Word of God gives many characteristics of faith.

Faith is substance and evidence (Hebrews 11:1).

- o It can be seen (Luke 5:20).
- o It be heard (Galatians 3:2).

Faith is quantitative.

- o It is great (Matthew 8:10).
- o It can be as small as a mustard seed (Luke 17:6).
- o It is little (Matthew 16:8).

Faith is alive.

- o It is alive with works (action) (James 2:20).
- o It comes and grows (Romans 10:17; Galatians 3:25).

Faith is a decision (Joshua 24:15; Deuteronomy 30:19).

- • You must decide to accept and trust what you feel in your heart.

Faith is a gift.

- o It is authored by God (Hebrews 12:2).
- o It is measured by God and given to every person (Romans 12:3).

How does faith work? Whenever faith is verbally expressed, your faith is "quickened," or made alive. The power of God is activated and made available. The confidence of the one speaking it, as well as those who hear it, increases. "So then faith cometh by hearing, and hearing by the word of God" (Romans 10:17). Notice it doesn't say it comes from having heard it in the past or hearing about it occasionally. Faith will come and increase when the Word of God is continually heard.

Faith is the substance of things hoped for.
Faith is the substance of things.
Faith is the substance!
Faith is substance!
Faith is the evidence of things not seen (Hebrews 11:1).

> Faith is the evidence of things.
> Faith is the evidence!
> Faith is evidence!

Let's look at nature for a moment. In nature, numerous chemical reactions occur regularly, as designed by God. Under certain conditions, a reaction takes place between the catalyst and another element. The outcome of that reaction often produces a new substance or a change from the original state of being. Faith works similarly. Faith is a supernatural force that activates the power of God, as it is directed. Faith is the catalyst that activates the power of God and releases the rivers of living water (Holy Spirit) that flow out of our bellies to heal, set free, and deliver (John 7:38). This means the people possessing the catalyst of faith also possess the ability to change situations and circumstances for themselves and to whomever they are ministering.

Jesus said if you have faith the size of a tiny mustard seed, that quantity of faith is enough to move a mountain (Luke 17:6)! Signs should follow believers. Signs are unusual supernatural occurrences that have no natural explanation. Whenever God works a miracle for someone who has little or no faith of their own, it is a sign. It testifies of his existence and his sovereignty. God performs unexplainable miracles to demonstrate to humankind that he is all-powerful and in control. We're taking our healing by faith! We are submitting to God and resisting the devil with our faith (James 4:7). God sets the choice before us and says,

> I call heaven and earth to record this day against you, that I have set before you life and

death, blessing and cursing; therefore, choose life, that both thou and thy seed may live. (Deuteronomy 30:19)

God desires that we live and that we live life to the fullest. Jesus said, "I am come that you might have life and have it more abundantly" (John 10:10). This verse also lets us know that Satan, our adversary, takes advantage of this. He walks around as a roaring lion, seeking those he may devour. He is the thief who comes to steal, kill, and destroy our quality of life. Sin and the nature of sin create an entryway for sickness and disease to enter our bodies.

For the wages of sin is death; but the gift of God is eternal life through Jesus Christ our Lord. (Romans 6:23 KJV)

Jesus warned the man who had been paralyzed, saying,

Behold, thou art made whole: sin no more, lest a worse thing come on thee. (John 5:14, emphasis added)

Jesus also corrects scribes and Pharisees in Luke 5:23–24.

Whether is easier, to say, Thy sins be forgiven thee; or to say, Rise up and walk? But that ye may know that the Son of man hath power upon earth to forgive sins, (he said unto the sick of the palsy,) I say unto thee, Arise, and take up thy couch, and go into thine house.

Beloved, we also have a role in the state and condition of our temples. We should take care of ourselves, live holy, and be good stewards of our bodies.

> What? Know ye not that your body is the temple of the Holy Ghost which is in you. Which ye have of God. And you are not your own. (1 Corinthians 6:19)

We should strive to walk in divine health and settle for nothing less. God prepared the "good" of life for us before we were born, and the Father enjoys giving it to us! Psalm 84:11b says, "No good thing will he withhold from them that walk uprightly." Jesus also told us in the book of Luke,

> Fear not, little flock, for it is your Father's good pleasure to give you the kingdom. (Luke 12:32)

The apostles Peter and John demonstrated how we should also be a blessing to others. When the apostles ministered to the man at the gate called Beautiful, they were confident that the virtue they had inside them would be a blessing to the man who was begging before them. In the book of Acts 3, Peter and John looked at the man with boldness and confidence as the power of God flowed through them, out of their bellies (their spirits), as a river of living water. They told him to look at them.

> Then Peter said, Silver and gold have I none; but such as I have give I thee: In the name of Jesus Christ of Nazareth rise up and walk. (Acts 3:6)

Peter and John were communicating to him through their actions that what they had inside them was more valuable than money. They loaned him their faith, and he was instantly healed and carried his bed, rejoicing.

We don't have to live with sickness and disease. We are healed by the stripes of our Savior, Jesus Christ (1 Peter 2:24). It was prophesied in Isaiah 53:4–5:

> Surely he hath borne our griefs, carried our sorrows, yet we did esteem him stricken, smitten of God, and afflicted. But he was wounded for our transgressions. He was bruised for our iniquities. The chastisement of our peace was upon him, and with his stripes we are healed.

Our healing has been bought and paid for by our Lord and Savior, Jesus Christ. It is part of the atonement that Jesus paid for us on the cross.

> The law of the Spirit of life in Christ Jesus hath made me free from the law of sin and death. (Romans 8:2)

We access this benefit through our faith.

CHAPTER 2

A Victorious Mentality

What's on Your Mind?

Do you maintain a victorious mentality? A victorious mentality is full of hope and optimism. When you or a loved one experiences sickness and disease, your attention is directed on the pain and suffering, instead of the precious promises of healing in the Word of God. Our thoughts control our behavior and our conversations; therefore, it is vital that we stay focused on the Word of God. Remember that we serve El Shaddai, the Lord God Almighty. He is Elohim, our Creator, and Jehovah Rapha, the Lord who heals us (Exodus 15:26).

> Ye are of God, little children, and have overcome them: because greater is he that is in you, than he that is in the world. (1 John 4:4)

We have a victorious mentality because Jesus lives inside of us.

> For as he thinketh in his heart, so is he ...
> (Proverbs 23:7a)

We must see ourselves as God sees us and stand on his Word. Don't keep changing your mind. Settle your faith in your spirit, and don't allow negative thoughts to move you.

> A double minded man is unstable in all his ways. (James 1:8).

Leave no room for doubt because doubt blocks you from receiving the blessing.

> For let not that man think that he shall receive any thing of the Lord. (James 1:7)

The Good Fight

We must always protect what comes in through our ear gates. What we hear will affect what and how we think and, ultimately, what we believe. Whenever you experience symptoms or receive negative medical information from a health care provider, acknowledge the facts and target your faith. Guard your heart. Don't listen to Satan and his lies whenever he comes to you and tries to convince you that you're not healed. Submit to God, and resist Satan. Resist him means refuse to listen to him, and don't allow negative thoughts to linger on your mind.

In chapter 5 of the Gospel of Luke, we see an example of teamwork and a determined mindset. Four friends believed that Jesus could heal their friend. They took action, overcame obstacles, and accessed the healing power of

God for their friend! We will talk about their "visible faith" in chapter 3.

In Luke 5:20, Jesus said unto him, "Man, thy sins are forgiven thee." In Luke 5:23, Jesus explained, "Whether is easier, to say, thy sins be forgiven thee, or to say rise up and walk?" Jesus was teaching us that whenever the power of God is present, all things are possible with God. The same power and faith that saved your soul is the power and faith that heals your body. If you believe that you're saved, then you should also believe that you're healed because healing is a kingdom benefit, as stated in Psalm 103:

> Bless the Lord, O my soul, and forget not all of
> His benefits, who forgiveth all thine iniquities;
> who healeth all thy diseases; Who redeemeth
> thy life from destruction; who crowneth thee
> with lovingkindness and tender mercies. (Psalm
> 103:2–4)

Hold fast to your profession of faith, and trust Jehovah Rapha. In other words, keep speaking faith-filled words; moreover, keep speaking the Word of God. The apostle Paul encouraged Pastor Timothy to avoid strife and carnality and to aggressively pursue eternal life and his faith (1 Timothy 6:12–13). God "quickens" all things; this means God "makes alive" all things! Healing is a kingdom benefit that is available to us daily (Psalm 103). God the Father loves his children, and he wants us to be well. He said "no good thing would he withhold from them that walk uprightly" (Psalm 84:11). When you are in need of a miracle, you can't quit. Stay in the faith race. It's a marathon, not a sprint. Run, walk, or crawl if you have to, but stay in the race of faith. The devil will get tired of waiting for you to quit, and he'll flee. Make up your mind and be determined! Doubt is your enemy—give it no place in your thoughts. First Corinthians 15:58 exhorts us to "be steadfast, unmovable, always abounding in the work of the Lord, knowing that your work is not in vain."

Don't lose your momentum of faith by taking a break. Keep studying and praying the Word so that your faith continues to grow. As a result, long-suffering, a fruit of the spirit, will begin to develop in your life. Be determined to outlast your enemy.

> But he that shall endure unto the end, the same shall be saved. (Matthew 24:13)

> Submit yourselves therefore to God. Resist the devil, and he will flee from you. (James 4:7)

> Watch ye, stand fast in the faith, quit you like men, be strong. (1 Corinthians 16:13)

Don't rely on your strength or lean to your own understanding. Fight the good fight, as described in Ephesians:

> Finally, my brethren, be strong in the Lord, and in the power of his might. For we wrestle not against flesh and blood, but against principalities, against powers, against the rulers of the darkness of this world, against spiritual wickedness in high places. Wherefore take unto you the whole armor of God, that ye may be able withstand in the evil

day, and having done all, to stand. (Ephesians 6:10–13)

The Abundant Life

God desires the best for us. He is concerned about how we are living, even down to the minute details! Matthew 10:30 tells us that the very hairs on our heads are numbered—that's how valuable we are to God.

> The thief cometh not, but for to steal, and to kill, and to destroy: I am come that they might have life, and that they might have it more abundantly. (John 10:10 KJV)

Jesus came to make the abundant life available to us, but we do have a role to play. We have to fight the good fight of faith. Why is it a fight? Because we have a jealous adversary.

> And from the days of John the Baptist until now the kingdom of heaven suffereth violence, and the violent take it by force. (Matthew 11:12 KJV)

As citizens in God's kingdom, we fight for righteousness, peace, and joy. What are we taking by force? Life—we choose the abundant life!

Let's look at an example from the Word of God, when those in need of healing ditched the "victim, poor me, why me?" mentality and decided to do something. In the book of 2 Kings 7, we find the story of the four lepers.

If we say, we will enter into the city, then the famine is in the city, and we shall die there: and if we sit still here, we die also. [They encouraged each other to take a risk and do something.] Now; therefore come, and let us fall unto the host of the Syrians: if they save us alive, we shall live; and if they kill us, we shall but die. And they rose up [They took action] in the twilight, to go unto the camp of the Syrians: and when they were come to the uttermost part of the camp of Syria, behold, there was no man there. For the Lord had made the host of the Syrians to hear a noise of chariots [God intervened and performed a miracle], and a noise of horses, even the noise of a great host: and they said one to another, Lo, the king of Israel hath hired against us the kings of the Hittites, and the kings of the Egyptians, to come upon us. And when these lepers came to the uttermost part of the camp, they went into one tent, and did eat and drink, and carried thence silver, and gold, and raiment [The lepers got blessed!], and went and hid it; and came again, and entered into another tent, and carried thence also, and went and hid it. (2 Kings 7:3–6)

These four lepers had to live an isolated life away from family and society. They were afflicted with an incurable, painful, disfiguring, and highly contagious disease, yet they did not give up. They easily could have felt sorry for themselves, but they did not have a pity party. We should follow their example. We can learn from the five things they did:

1. They encouraged one another (2 Kings 7:4).
2. They devised a plan of positive action (2 Kings 7:4).
3. They did something (2 Kings 7:5).
4. They improved their situation (2 Kings 7:8).
5. They created a victory for the king (2 Kings 7:15).

Self-Evaluation: Are you taking positive actions to keep your faith alive?

> But wilt thou know, O vain man, that faith without works is dead? (James 2:20)

Now let's take a look at the story in the 5th chapter of the gospel of John about the man at the pool of Bethesda. His story teaches that how you view yourself and your situation will affect your outcome.

> After this there was a feast of the Jews; and Jesus went up to Jerusalem. Now there is at Jerusalem by the sheep market a pool, which is called in the Hebrew tongue Bethesda, having five porches. In these lay a great multitude of impotent folk, of blind, halt, withered, waiting for the moving of the water. For an angel went down at a certain season into the pool, and troubled the water: whosoever then first after the troubling of the water stepped in was made whole of whatsoever disease he had. And a certain man was there, which had an infirmity thirty and eight years. When Jesus saw him lie, and knew that he had been now a long time in that case, he saith unto him, Wilt thou be made whole? The impotent man answered

> him, Sir, I have no man, when the water is
> troubled, to put me into the pool: but while I
> am coming, another steppeth down before me.
> Jesus saith unto him, Rise, take up thy bed,
> and walk. (John 5:1–8)

There are many opinions of why the man was lying at the pool for thirty-eight long years. Was he lazy? Was he paralyzed? Did he really want to be made whole? When Jesus approached the man, he was moved with compassion. Jesus realized that because the man had been in that condition for a long time, he would not only need a physical change but a change in his mentality also. Therefore, he asked him, "Will you be made whole?" Jesus was offering the man the opportunity to change, if that was what he truly desired. Jesus was stirring up faith in the man to believe that he could be healed. It's important. Do you visualize yourself healed? It is necessary so that once the physical change takes place in your body, your faith and mentality will maintain it.

> For as he thinketh in his heart, so is he.
> (Proverbs 23:7a)

My question to you is this: What are you hoping for? No matter the situation or circumstance, no matter the diagnosis or prognosis, keep hope alive! Your faith is the substance (the tangible, visible material) of what you are hoping and verbally praying for.

In other words, your faith transforms your hopes and dreams into reality. That's right—I said dreams! Dreams are visual.

If you can see yourself whole, then you can believe yourself whole. Your reality is according to your faith.

Self-Evaluation: Do you have enough faith for yourself and for someone else? Do you make excuses to explain the lack of progress? Do you have a plan of action?

CHAPTER 3

It's According to Your Faith!

Faith is the supernatural force that powers the kingdom of God. By faith, the worlds were framed, and without it, it is impossible to please God. The just shall live by faith, the dead are raised by faith, and the sick are recovered by faith. What you receive and how fast you receive it depends on your faith level. Jesus only marveled at the faith of three people, and all three were Gentiles.

In this chapter, we will study several healing miracles: the tenth leper, the man sick of the palsy, the centurion soldier's servant, and the Syrophoenician woman's daughter.

Grateful Faith: The Tenth Leper

> And as he entered into a certain village, there met him ten men that were lepers, which stood afar off: And they lifted up their voices,

and said, Jesus, Master, have mercy on us.
And when he saw them, he said unto them,
Go shew yourselves unto the priests. And it
came to pass, that, as they went, they were
cleansed. And one of them, when he saw that
he was healed, turned back, and with a loud
voice glorified God, And fell down on his face
at his feet, giving him thanks: and he was a
Samaritan. And Jesus answering said, Were
there not ten cleansed? but where are the nine?
There are not found that returned to give glory
to God, save this stranger. And he said unto
him, Arise, go thy way: thy faith hath made
thee whole. (Luke 17:10–19)

In this story, ten lepers were desperate for a healing touch
from God. Destiny presented them with a chance to receive
their healing when Jesus entered their village. They cried for
him to have mercy upon them and grant their request to be
made whole. Jesus answered their request by giving a simple
command: "Go present yourselves to the priest and take the
specified offering." Selah.

Do we come to God empty-handed? Selah.

They obeyed the command and were cleansed as they went. But
only one out of the ten recognized that they weren't speaking
to a mere man but to God himself. The tenth leper glorified
God and fell down and worshipped him. His recognition of
the power of God and his obedience to the man of God was
equated to faith. Jesus said, "Thy faith hath made thee whole"
(Luke 17:15; 2:2–5).

Visible Faith—The Man Sick of the Palsy (Mark 2:2–5)

> And straightway many were gathered together, insomuch that there was no room to receive them, no, not so much as about the door: and he preached the word unto them. And they come unto him, bringing one sick of the palsy, which was borne of four. And when they could not come nigh unto him for the press, they uncovered the roof where he was: and when they had broken it up, they let down the bed wherein the sick of the palsy lay. When Jesus saw their faith, he said unto the sick of the palsy, Son, thy sins be forgiven thee.

Jesus saw their faith—they expressed their faith by their actions. They went through extraordinary lengths to get their friend to Jesus. The person being healed said and did nothing! He was the benefactor of someone else's faith.

Beyond Faith—A Knowing: The Woman with the Issue of Blood (Mark 5:25)

The Word of God is full of examples of healings, miracles, signs, and wonders that occurred in the ministry of Jesus. Although the faith level of the recipients varied, the power of God was present to heal, and Jesus went about doing good and healing all who were oppressed of the devil (Acts 10:38),

Next, let's review Mark 5:25-28, the story of the woman with the issue of blood. Verse 25 states that she suffered with this condition for twelve years, yet still had faith that she could and would be healed. According to the law, a woman with a menstrual bleed was considered unclean and was not allowed to be out in public. But her desperation and her belief in the power of Jesus and his ability to heal her caused her to risk being exposed, just to get a touch. Her faith gave her the courage to take action. She positioned herself to receive the power of God. *Are you in position to receive God's virtue?* She dismissed all doubts and focused her faith. She touched the hem of His garment which became the point of contact through which the power of god flowed. Jesus explained to her that her faith made this miracle manifest.

> For she said within herself, If I may but touch his garment, I shall be whole. But Jesus turned him about, and when he saw her, he said, Daughter, be of good comfort; thy faith hath made thee whole. And the woman was made whole from that hour. (Matthew 9:21–22)

Her faith was great because she understood that virtue was flowing in his garment, power to end 12 years of chronic disease. Because her faith level was high, she didn't need him to pray for or lay hands on her. If she could just touch his clothes, she knew that there was enough virtue in his clothing to make her whole.

Do you need a touch from the Lord? Do you believe? Whether chronic or acute, the power of God will make you whole!

The next example I want to highlight is found in Matthew 9:27 Jesus was followed by two blind men who were crying and pleading for Jesus to heal them. Jesus tested their faith level in verse 28 and acted on their faith in verse29. Jesus asked them if they had faith to believe that he was able to heal them. They verbally acknowledged their faith and reverenced his authority by calling him Lord.

> Then touched he their eyes, saying, according to your faith, be it unto you. And their eyes were opened. And Jesus? straightly charged them, saying, see that no man know it. (Matthew 9:28-30)

Do you verbally acknowledge your faith? Do you reverence his name?

> The name of the Lord is a strong tower. The righteous run into it and they are safe. (Proverbs 18:10)

Steadfast Faith: The Syrophoenician Woman

> And, behold, a woman of Canaan came out of the same coasts, and cried unto him, saying, Have mercy on me, O Lord, thou Son of David; my daughter is grievously vexed with a devil. ... Then came she and worshipped him, saying, Lord, help me But he answered and said, It is not meet to take the children's bread, and to cast it to dogs. And she said, Truth, Lord: yet the dogs eat of the crumbs which fall from their masters' table. (Matthew 15:22, 25–27)

In Matthew 15:28 Jesus told the woman, "Great is thy faith." The writer, Apostle Matthew, focused on the woman's faith and how she prepared herself to receive her miracle. Jesus used the word great to describe it. He gave it a value, a quantitative measure. She didn't just have faith; her faith had a different quality. Her faith had a great quality when compared to everyone else. The word of God describes faith as "little, great, much, the size of a mustard seed, strong" to name a few adjectives. This lets us know that there are different levels, qualities and quantities of faith. She received a great miracle because she possessed and exercised great faith.

The power of God is not limited by time and space. Her daughter, who was in a different location, was healed immediately. No hands were laid on her. No prayer was offered for her. But Jesus took authority over the evil spirit. God's power responded to her faith and caused his power to be activated in her daughter's life from that very moment.

Our faith quickens (makes active) his power!

> I have set before thee this day life and good, and death and evil. (Deuteronomy 30:15)

> For the law of the Spirit of life in Christ Jesus hath made me free from the law of sin and death. (Romans 8:2)

Steadfast Faith: The Syrophoenician Woman, part 2

> For a certain woman, whose young daughter had an unclean spirit, heard of him, and came and fell at his feet: The woman was a Greek,

a Syrophoenician by nation; and she besought him that he would cast forth the devil out of her daughter. But Jesus said unto her, "Let the children first be filled: for it is not meet to take the children's bread, and to cast it unto the dogs. And she answered and said unto him, Yes, Lord: yet the dogs under the table eat of the children's crumbs. And he said unto her, For this saying go thy way; the devil is gone out of thy daughter. And when she was come to her house, she found the devil gone out, and her daughter laid upon the bed. (Mark 8:25–30)

Mark 8:25 shows us that she believed that Jesus had the power to help her daughter and change the situation. We should learn three things from her: humility, wisdom, and active faith.

First lesson: humility.

Take notice of how she approached Jesus. She realized that she was not a part of the Jewish community. She recognized that she was coming before a man of greatness; therefore, she humbled herself at his feet. Her attitude was completely opposite of Naaman's. (Read the story of the army commander afflicted with leprosy in the book of Isaiah.) She realized she was requesting a benefit that was not due her. But she had the faith to try because she was convinced that Jesus had the power to help her.

Second lesson: wisdom.

Her humility allowed her not to be insulted by Jesus's comparing her to a dog. Instead, she used the wisdom that she had to respond to him in the context of his own parable.

Third lesson: active faith.

This woman of Canaan put her faith into action by approaching Jesus against all odds.

She accepted the risk of rejection and embarrassment in order to get help for her daughter. It wasn't a matter of whether he could help her. It was just a matter of making the request. Her faith was activated, and it compelled her to act.

Do you feel compelled enough to act in your situation or circumstance? Selah.

She humbled herself and fell at Jesus's feet. She accepted the initial comparison to a dog and his initial denial of her request. She was determined and unmovable—and full of wisdom. She was able to make a reasonable response to Jesus using his own parable. The blessing of the Lord she was seeking was healing for her daughter. She did not argue with the Man of God. She simply humbled herself and received. Notice that Jesus declared to her that "for this saying," her daughter has been made whole (verse 20). He said, "For this saying go thy way."

In other words, because of what you said, I'm granting your request. Even though you aren't of the House of Israel, I'm overriding that stipulation because of your faith. He called her faith great in Matthew 15:28a—"Woman, great is thy faith. Therefore, I'm granting your request and you will have what you want."

Her prayer was answered immediately. The next miracle was a long-distance one, and it was a result of intercession to the Savior for someone else's healing.

Great Faith: The Centurion Soldier

> And a certain centurion's servant, who was dear unto him, was sick, and ready to die. And when he heard of Jesus, he sent unto him the elders of the Jews, beseeching him that he would come and heal his servant. And when they came to Jesus, they besought him instantly, saying, That he was worthy for whom he should do this: For he loveth our nation, and he hath built us a synagogue. Then Jesus went with them. And when he was now not far from the house, the centurion sent friends to him, saying unto him, Lord, trouble not thyself: for I am not worthy that thou shouldest enter under my roof: Wherefore neither thought I myself worthy to come unto thee: but say in a word, and my servant shall be healed.
>
> For I also am a man set under authority, having under me soldiers, and I say unto one, Go, and he goeth; and to another, Come, and he cometh; and to my servant, Do this, and he doeth it. When Jesus heard these things, he marveled at him, and turned him about, and said unto the people that followed him, I say unto you, I have not found so great faith, no, not in Israel. (Luke 7:2–9)

It is evident that the centurion had faith in God before this miracle because he was a donor to the synagogue, not a usual thing for a Roman soldier to do. The centurion's faith was strong because he recognized the spiritual authority with which Jesus was ministering, and he respected Jesus's power. He believed that Jesus's power could transcend time and space; therefore, it was only necessary for Jesus to authorize the healing in order for it to take place.

> And they that were sent, returning to the house,
> found the servant whole that had been sick.
> (Luke 7:10)

So, it happened the way he believed it would, according to his faith.

CHAPTER 4

It's According to Your Words

What are you saying? Remember we will be judged for every idle word we speak.

> But I say unto you, that every idle word that men shall speak, they shall give account thereof in the day of judgment. (Matthew 12:36)

Our words determine what our outcomes will be.

> A man shall eat good by the fruit of his mouth: but the soul of the transgressors shall eat violence. He that keepeth his mouth keepeth his life: but he that openeth wide his lips shall have destruction. (Proverbs 13:2–3)

God has given us the ability to determine our own destiny by what we say.

> Death and life are in the power of the tongue:
> and they that love it shall eat the fruit thereof.
> (Proverbs 18:21)

God responds based on what we say. In the beginning of Isaiah 57:19, God tells us clearly, "I create the fruit of the lips." So speak life!

Our words activate God's will to come
to pass on earth as it is in heaven.

We Are Free!

Beloved, we are no longer bound by the fall of man in the garden. We have been redeemed by the blood of the Lamb, Jesus Christ, our Lord. Therefore, we have been made free!

> For the law of the Spirit of life in Christ Jesus
> hath made me free from the law of sin and
> death. (Romans 8:2)

God's power is available on demand. He's waiting for us to take dominion over that sickness and disease. Take authority over negative circumstance. Walk in your God-given authority of a born-again believer.

When you became a born-again believer, your position changed in the realm of the spirit. We are now seated with Christ in heavenly places. We're above only and not beneath. Therefore, we should look down on negative circumstances and realize that we are above only. Now we soar above them!

All we have to do is accept the Word of God and speak it over ourselves. We are to speak it into existence the same way God Elohim created the earth and everything in it. If you are a believer, your words have creative power because you were made in his image and after his likeness.

When we speak of ourselves as the Word says about us, the logos Word of God becomes the rhema word, alive and active.

> For the word of God is quick, and powerful, and sharper than any two-edged sword, piercing even to the dividing asunder of soul and spirit, and of the joints and marrow, and is a discerner of the thoughts and intents of the heart. (Hebrews 4:12)

> It is the spirit that quickeneth; the flesh profiteth nothing: the words that I speak unto you, they are spirit, and they are life. (John 6:63)

Speak life over your body! Call those things that are not as if they were. Call situations as you want them to be. Declare your desired outcome. Talk the solution, the resolution, not the problem or the attack. Decree and declare that you are whole and entire, and you lack nothing! Declare that this sickness is not unto death, that you will live and not die, and declare the works of the Lord.

You've heard the saying, "adding fuel to the fire." Well, we don't want to add any fuel to the enemy's fire against us.

Instead, add faith. Faith will empower the ministering spirits, the angels, to war on our behalf and to bring us messages and gifts from Jehovah Rapha, our healer. Realize that your battle is only temporary. This too shall pass. The test didn't come to stay; it came to pass.

The power is in your mouth! Our mouths are spiritual doors to the supernatural spirit realm. When our faith-filled words are spoken, they produce sound waves charged with the power of God, which works in us. These sound waves move atoms and molecules to cause situations and circumstances to line up in accordance with the with the words of our commands or prayers. This the reason why Jesus said, it's not what goes into me that defiles me but what comes out. I believe that the words that proceed from our mouth are the "living water" that proceeds from the throne of God.

> The words of a man's mouth are as deep waters in the wellspring of wisdom as the flowing brook. (Proverbs 18:4)

> God says "I am the fountain of living waters." (Jeremiah 2:13)

> And he showed me a pure river of water, of life clear as crystal, proceeding out of the throne of God and out of the Lamb. (Revelation 22:1)

> He who believes on me out of his heart shall flow rivers of living water. (John 7:37)

If you abide in me and my words abide in you, you shall ask what you will [what you want or need], and it shall be done for you. (John 15:7)

If you shall ask anything in my name, I will do it. (John 14:14)

CHAPTER 5

Some Tools

Prayers and Scriptures to Increase Your Faith
and Cause Wholeness in Your Life
I call them my "daily dose of God's medicine."

TOOL 1

I received the following profession from the Holy Spirit on
February 18, 2020, while on a plane to Miami.

Prayer Profession for Wholeness

And the Just Shall Live by Faith—The key to a healthy life is
faith!

By faith, I believe that miracles, signs, and wonders are
occurring in my life.

By faith, I decree by the power vested in me by the Lord Jesus Christ that my body and it's more than eleven operating systems—digestive, immune, circulatory, integumentary, reproductive, respiratory, central nervous, endocrine, excretory, musculoskeletal, autonomic nervous, and limbic system—are fully functional and operating according to his divine design.

By faith, I declare and boldly say that there are no deficiencies in my body. I have homeostasis, and my equilibrium is steady and steadfast! My body chemistry is stable and at the proper levels and ratios.

By faith, my vision is sharp, and my visual acuity is 20/20. My cornea, retinas, lenses, pupils, eyelids, and inner eye components are free of damage or disease, stress or strain.

By faith, I proclaim that my blood is pure. It doesn't contain toxins, carcinogens, or excessive levels of lipids or glucose. My cells are not resistant to insulin. My liver and kidneys properly filter my blood continuously.

By faith, I decree that my body will reject all mutant, abnormal, precancerous or cancerous cells that may try to form. I declare that those foreign cells will not be able to plant themselves, thrive, or survive in my body.

The power of the Most High God permeates every cell, fiber, tissue, and organ of my body, forming a protective force field that Satan and the forces of darkness cannot penetrate. I am supernaturally covered and protected by the blood of Jesus! The faith-filled words of my mouth activate this force field and keep it operative.

By faith, the elders obtained a good report!

By faith, I report that my health springs forth speedily and manifests in my body swiftly, with notable, undeniable miracles and divine interventions of the Most High God.

By faith, I decree and speak to my [area of attack, specific body part or organ, process, or function], and I declare by faith that I am healed, recovered, and fully restored.

By faith, I command_[sickness or disease] to cease and desist its operations in my body. It is under divine arrest. It can progress no further in the name of Jesus!

Praise the Lord!

TOOL 2

101 Things God Said (about Healing)[1]

How do we know whether it's God's will to heal us or not? It makes little difference what others say about it. What did He say about it? Remember that God is no respecter of persons (Acts 10: 34), and He never changes (Malachi 3:6). So what He said to them yesterday, He is saying to you today. God's Word is God speaking to me. (These statements are taken directly from the Bible with little or no variation. The verbs and construction have been changed to apply to you personally and to sum up the thoughts in some instances. Also, many of these statements are prefaced by phrases like, "If you walk in My commandments," "If you believe … obey …" etc.)

---

[1] Keith Moore, "God's Will to Heal" (Faith Life Publishing, 2013).

1. I am the Lord that healeth thee (Exodus 15:26).
2. Your days shall be one hundred and twenty years (Genesis 6:3).
3. You shall be buried in a good old age (Genesis 15:15).
4. You shall come to your grave in a full age like as a shock of corn cometh in his season (Job 5:26).
5. When I see the blood, I will pass over you and the plague shall not be upon you to destroy you (Exodus 12:13).
6. I will take sickness away from the midst of you and the number of your days I will fulfill (Exodus 23:25, 26).
7. I will not put any of the diseases you are afraid of on you, but I will take all sickness away from you (Deuteronomy 7:15).
8. It will be well with you and your days shall be multiplied and prolonged as the days of heaven upon the earth (Deuteronomy 11:9, 21).
9. I turned the curse into a blessing unto you, because I loved you (Deuteronomy 23:5 and Nehemiah 13:2).
10. I have redeemed you from every sickness and every plague (Deuteronomy 28:61 and Galatians 3:13).
11. As your days, so shall your strength be (Deuteronomy 33:25).
12. I have found a ransom for you, your flesh shall be fresher than a child's and you shall return to the days of your youth (Job 33:24–25).
13. I have healed you and brought up your soul from the grave; I have kept you alive from going down into the pit (Psalm 30:1–2).
14. I will give you strength and bless you with peace (Psalm 29:11).
15. I will preserve you and keep you alive (Psalm 41:2).

16. I will strengthen you upon the bed of languishing; I will turn all your bed in your sickness (Psalm 41:3).

17. I am the health of your countenance and your God (Psalm 43:5).

18. No plague shall come near your dwelling (Psalm 91:10).

19. I will satisfy you with long life (Psalm 91:16).

20. I heal all your diseases (Psalm 103:3).

21. I sent My word and healed you and delivered you from your destructions (Psalm 107:20).

22. You shall not die, but live, and declare My works (Psalm 118:17).

23. I heal your broken heart and bind up your wounds (Psalm 147:3).

24. The years of your life shall be many (Proverbs 4:10).

25. Trusting Me brings health to your navel and marrow to your bones (Proverbs 3:8).

26. My words are life to you, and health/medicine to all your flesh (Proverbs 4:22).

27. (My) good report makes your bones fat (Proverbs 15:30).

28. (My) pleasant words are sweet to your soul and health to your bones (Proverbs 16:24).

29. My joy is your strength. A merry heart does good like a medicine (Nehemiah 8:10; Proverbs 17:22).

30. The eyes of the blind shall be opened. The eyes of them that see shall not be dim (Isaiah 32:3; 35:5).

31. The ears of the deaf shall be unstopped. The ears of them that hear shall hearken (Isaiah 32:3; 35:5).

32. The tongue of the dumb shall sing. The tongue of the stammerers shall be ready to speak plainly (Isaiah 35:6; 32:4).

33. The lame man shall leap as a hart (Isaiah 35:6).
34. I will recover you and make you to live. I am ready to save you (Isaiah 38:16, 20).
35. I give power to the faint. I increase strength to them that have no might (Isaiah 40:29).
36. I will renew your strength. I will strengthen and help you (Isaiah 40:31; 41:10).
37. To your old age and gray hairs I will carry you and I will deliver you (Isaiah 46:4).
38. I bore your sickness (Isaiah 53:4).
39. I carried your pains (Isaiah 53:4).
40. I was put to sickness for you (Isaiah 53:10).
41. With My stripes you are healed (Isaiah 53:5).
42. I will heal you (Isaiah 57:19).
43. Your light shall break forth as the morning and your health shall spring forth speedily (Isaiah 58:8).
44. I will restore health unto you, and I will heal you of your wounds saith the Lord (Jeremiah 30:17).
45. Behold I will bring it health and cure, and I will cure you, and will reveal unto you the abundance of peace and truth (Jeremiah 33:6).
46. I will bind up that which was broken and will strengthen that which was sick (Ezekiel 34:16).
47. Behold, I will cause breath to enter into you and you shall live. And I shall put My Spirit in you and you shall live (Ezekiel 37:5, 14).
48. Whithersoever the rivers shall come shall live. They shall be healed and everything shall live where the river comes (Ezekiel 47:9).
49. Seek Me and you shall live (Amos 5:4, 6).
50. I have arisen with healing in My wings (beams) (Malachi 4:2).

51. I will, be thou clean (Matthew 8:3).
52. I took your infirmities (Matthew 8:17).
53. I bore your sicknesses (Matthew 8:17).
54. If you're sick you need a physician. (I am the Lord your physician) (Matthew 9:12 and Exodus 15:26).
55. I am moved with compassion toward the sick and I heal them (Matthew 14:14).
56. I heal all manner of sickness and all manner of disease (Matthew 4:23).
57. According to your faith, be it unto you (Matthew 9:29).
58. I give you power and authority over all unclean spirits to cast them out, and to heal all manner of sickness and all manner of disease (Matthew 10:1 and Luke 9:1).
59. I heal them all (Matthew 12:15 and Hebrews 13:8).
60. As many as touch Me are made perfectly whole (Matthew 14:36).
61. Healing is the children's bread (Matthew 15:26).
62. I do all things well. I make the deaf to hear and the dumb to speak (Mark 7:37).
63. If you can believe, all things are possible to him that believeth (Mark 9:23; 11:23–24).
64. When hands are laid on you, you shall recover (Mark 16:18).
65. My anointing heals the brokenhearted, and delivers the captives, recovers sight to the blind, and sets at liberty those that are bruised (Luke 4:18; Isaiah 10:27; 61:1).
66. I heal all those who have need of healing (Luke 9:11).
67. I am not come to destroy men's lives but to save them (Luke 9:56).
68. Behold, I give you authority over all the enemy's power and nothing shall by any means hurt you (Luke 10:19).

69. Sickness is satanic bondage and you ought to be loosed today (Luke 13:16; 2 Corinthians 6:2).

70. In Me is life (John 1:4).

71. I am the bread of life. I give you life (John 6:33, 35).

72. The words I speak unto you are spirit and life (John 6:63).

73. I am come that you might have life, and that you might have it more abundantly (John 10:10).

74. I am the resurrection and the life (John 11:25).

75. If you ask anything in My name, I will do it (John 14:14).

76. Faith in My name makes you strong and gives you perfect soundness (Acts 3:16).

77. I stretch forth My hand to heal (Acts 4:30).

78. I, Jesus Christ, make you whole (Acts 9:34).

79. I do good and heal all that are oppressed of the devil (Acts 10:38).

80. My power causes diseases to depart from you (Acts 19:12).

81. The law of the Spirit of life in Me has made you free from the law of sin and death (Romans 8:2).

82. The same Spirit that raised Me from the dead now lives in you and that Spirit will quicken your mortal body (Romans 8:11).

83. Your body is a member of Me (1 Corinthians 6:15).

84. Your body is the temple of My Spirit and you're to glorify Me in your body (1 Corinthians 6:19–20).

85. If you'll rightly discern My body which was broken for you, and judge yourself, you'll not be judged and you'll not be weak, sickly or die prematurely (1 Corinthians 11:29–31).

86. I have set gifts of healing in My body (1 Corinthians 12:9).

87. My life may be made manifest in your mortal flesh (2 Corinthians 4:10–11).
88. I have delivered you from death, I do deliver you, and if you trust Me I will yet deliver you (2 Corinthians 1:10).
89. I have given you My name and have put all things under your feet (Ephesians 1:21–22).
90. I want it to be well with you and I want you to live long on the earth. (Ephesians 6:3).
91. I have delivered you from the authority of darkness (Colossians 1:13).
92. I will deliver you from every evil work (2 Timothy 4:18).
93. I tasted death for you. I destroyed the devil who had the power of death. I've delivered you from the fear of death and bondage (Hebrews 2:9, 14–15).
94. I wash your body with pure water (Hebrews 10:22; Ephesians 5:26).
95. Lift up the weak hands and the feeble knees. Don't let that which is lame be turned aside but rather let Me heal it (Hebrews 12:12–13).
96. Let the elders anoint you and pray for you in My name and I will raise you up (James 5:14–15).
97. Pray for one another and I will heal you (James 5:16).
98. By My stripes you were healed (1 Peter 2:24).
99. My Divine power has given unto you all things that pertain unto life and godliness through the knowledge of Me (2 Peter 1:3).
100. Whosoever will, let him come and take of the water of life freely (Revelation 22:17).
101. Beloved, I wish above all things that you may … be in health (3 John 2).

TOOL 3

Take a daily dose of God's medicine—His Word! Meditate on healing scriptures day and night.

And These Signs Shall Follow Them ...

> And these signs shall follow them that believe; In my name shall they cast out devils; they shall speak with new tongues; They shall take up serpents; and if they drink any deadly thing, it shall not hurt them; they shall lay hands on the sick, and they shall recover. (Mark 16:17–18)

Psalms: A Path to Healing and Deliverance

> The Lord is my shepherd: I shall not want, He maketh me to lie down in green pastures: he leadeth me beside the still waters, He restoreth my soul: he leadeth me in paths of righteousness for his name's sake. (Psalm 23:1–3)

> O Lord my God, I cried unto thee, and thou hast healed me. (Psalm 30:2)

> My covenant will I not break, nor alter the thing that is gone out of my lips. (Psalm 89:34)

> There shall no evil befall thee, neither shall any plague come nigh thy dwelling. (Psalm 91:10)

> With long life will I satisfy him and show him My salvation. (Psalm 91:16)

Bless the LORD, O my soul: and all that is within me, bless his holy name. Bless the LORD, O my soul, and forget not all his benefits: Who forgiveth all thine iniquities; who healeth all thy diseases; Who redeemeth thy life from destruction; who crowneth thee with lovingkindness and tender mercies. (Psalm 103:1–4)

He brought them forth also with silver and gold: and there was not one feeble person among their tribes. (Psalm 105:37)

Then they cry unto the Lord in their trouble, and he saveth them out of their distresses. (Psalm 107:19)

He sent his word and healed them and delivered them from their destructions. (Psalm 107:20)

I shall not die but live, and shall declare the works of the Lord. (Psalm 118:17)

Printed in the United States
by Baker & Taylor Publisher Services